WALKING IN THE LIGHT

When the Light (Jesus Christ) comes, darkness (Satanic power) disappears.

ACKNOWLEDGEMENT

It is impossible for a tree to make a forest. Therefore, to make this piece of work a success, a lot of 'forces' combined (together). **Please, compare Genesis 1:28; Psalm 127:1.**

God, the Maker of heavens and earth, through the power of the Holy Spirit supplied the materials (people, cash, ideas, etc) to accomplish this goal. **Please, compare John 14:26; Zechariah 4:6.**

In the light of these, I am thanking God Almighty for all those who contributed meaningfully, spiritually, or otherwise in the process of producing this book. This same God will supply all their needs according to His glory in Christ Jesus. Amen! **Please, compare 1st Corinthians 15:57; Philippians 4:19.**

PREFACE

"Your word is a lamp to my feet and a light to my path. Therefore, the entrance and unfolding of Your words give light; their unfolding gives understanding (discernment and comprehension) to the simple" – Psalm 119:105, 130.

"But you are a chosen race, a royal priesthood, a dedicated nation, [God's] own purchased, special people, that you may set forth the wonderful deeds and display the virtues and perfections of Him Who called you out of darkness into His marvelous light. Once you were not a people [at all], but now you are God's people; once you were un-pitied, but now you are pitied and have received mercy." Please, compare 1st Peter 2:9, 10.

"But if we [really] are living and walking in the Light, as He [Himself] is in the Light, we have [true, unbroken] fellowship with one another, and the blood of Jesus Christ His Son cleanses (removes) us from all sin and guilt [keeps us cleansed from sin in all its forms and manifestations]. Whoever says he is in the Light and [yet] hates his brother [Christian, born-again child of God his Father] is in darkness even until now." Please, compare 1st John 1:7; 2:9.

"Now, the sun shall no more be your light by day, nor for brightness shall the moon give light to you, but the Lord shall be to you an everlasting

light, and your God, your glory, and your beauty." Please, compare Isaiah 60:19.

"Blessed (Happy, fortunate, to be envied) are the undefiled (the upright, truly sincere, and blameless) in the way [of the revealed will of God], who walk (order their conduct and conversation) in the law of the Lord (the whole of God's revealed will). Therefore, I urge You Lord to establish my steps and direct them by [means of] Your word; let not any iniquity have dominion over me." Please, compare Psalm 119:1, 133.

"As a believer of Christ (who is walking in the light that has no shadow of turning), take no path in and have no fellowship with the fruitless deeds and enterprises of darkness, but instead [let your life be so in contrast as to] expose, reprove, and convict them. For, it is a shame even to speak of, or mention the things that [such people] practice in secret. But when anything is exposed and reproved by the light, it is made visible and clear; and where everything is visible and clear, there is light. Therefore, in that "glowing light", Jesus says, Awake, O sleeper, and arise from the dead, and Christ shall shine (make day dawn) upon you and give you light." Please, compare Ephesians 5:11-14; Isaiah 26:19; 60:1, 2.

TABLE OF CONTENTS

Preface	3
Introduction	6
Dedication	9
Chapter One: The Power of Change	10
Chapter Two: The Efficacy of Prayer	28
Chapter Three: Satan – Our Only Enemy	43
Chapter Four: God's Plan is not Man's Plan	61

INTRODUCTION

For everything that happens, there is always a reason or purpose. It has come to the notice of many that they are just living without knowing that their lives have meanings.

Why should a smoker, alcoholic, and a chemical drug user wakes up some day and grumble to the world that he is poor? He has failed to understand that doing the same thing all the time will produce the same results accordingly. Therefore, for him to know that his life is worth an immeasurable value to God and mankind, he has to change to allow God's will to manifest in his life.

How can we say we want to experience God's blessings without praying? Even God said: ***"Just as the night watch-men will not sleep until it is dawn, also we should not stop asking from Him until we are established." Please, compare Isaiah 62:6, 7.***

Have we ever seen a father giving a snake or scorpion to a child when the child asks for bread? If as cruelty as an earthly father can be so good to give good to his child, then, how is our heavenly Father who has loved us before we were created? Yes, He knows the thoughts He has for me; thoughts of good and not thoughts of evil. He assured me that these good thoughts will take me to His (delightful) end, beyond my expected end. **Please, compare Isaiah 49:15; Jeremiah 29:11.**

In everything, ask in prayer, supplications, and thanksgivings to God. You will always find if you seek from God. Prayer is the key that connects man to God.

The thief has come to steal, kill and destroy our joy, thereby leaving behind **"fear"** of not attaining the life God has planned for us. When Jesus Christ was to ascend to heaven, He said: *"... I have given you the power and authority to trample the lion, serpent, and scorpions... " Please, compare Matthew 28:18-20; John 19:30.*

At the mention of Christ's name, every knee shall bow – that is, all obstacles, disappointments, worries, etc., will be answerable to God's commands. Then, why are we in fear? **Please, compare Philippians 2:10, 11; John 16:33; Isaiah 54:15.**

For those who do not believe in the existence of Satan the Devil, there is a lot to learn about the world.

Satan, as an angel is more powerful, as he knows the intents of God more than the ordinary man! He has promised God that he would take over the earth, and deceive man not to discern on the truth of God. Therefore, today, when man does the will of Satan, he will be rewarded with satanic gains. Likewise, man will have God's blessings when he is adopted and adapted to God's divine principles. The only enemy to mankind is Satan the Devil.

Because we were created for God's glory, Satan became jealous, and used his trick of confidence to deceive man. Owing to God's love to mankind, He sacrificed His beloved Son on the Cross to exterminate the evil atrocities perpetrated by Satan in our lives. And anybody who wants to see the Father should come through Christ. Brethren, the only **"gift"** Satan cannot take away from you is the 'inner strength' of Christ – the **"Holy Spirit."** When that is lost to the devil, then you are under the influence of his (devil's) commands.

Because we are created for His glory and in His image, everything He has for us is good. It is man that has evil plans for man. However, when you know God and dwell in His presence, He will create a way when there seems to be no way. Is there anything impossible for God to do? He made the light and darkness; He made calamities and prosperities; poverty and riches; day and night; and so on. All we need is to look unto Him in all our desires. He is there to take us through waters without being drowned, or lead us through fire without being burnt.

My beloved brethren, as you read (or study) this book, you may learn to use the principles you find to walk in the light of God which have no shadow of turning. God bless you in Jesus name, Amen.

DEDICATION

This book is dedicated to the Holy Spirit

CHAPTER ONE

THE POWER OF CHANGE

"Repent, (think differently; change your mind, regretting your sins and changing your conduct), for the kingdom of God is at hand" – Matthew 3:2.

"Seek, inquire for, and require the Lord while He may be found [claiming Him by necessity and by right]; call upon Him while He is near. Let the wicked forsake his way and the unrighteous man his thoughts, and let him return to the Lord; and He will have love, pity, and mercy for him, and to our God, He will multiply to him His abundant pardon" – Prophet Isaiah 55:6, 7.

Romans 12:2 says, "Do not be conformed to this world (this age), [fashioned after and adapted to its external, superficial customs], but be transformed (changed) by the [entire] renewal of your mind [by its new ideals and its new attitude], so that you may prove [for yourselves] what is the good, acceptable and perfect will of God; even the thing which is good, acceptable and perfect [in His sight for you]."

WHAT IS CHANGE?

Change, in this respect, is merely a transformation from bad to good. That is to say, changing from what is unacceptable to God (somehow, tolerated by God), to what is required by God. **Galatians 6:7 says, *"Do not be deceived, deluded, and misled; God will not allow Himself to be sneered at (scorned, disdained, or mocked by mere pretensions or professions, or by His precepts being set aside). [He inevitably deceives himself who attempts to deceive God.] For whatever a man sows, that and that only is what he will reap."***

To buttress God's action and truthfulness, the fruits reaped from the disobedient seed sown by man were deaths (spiritual and physical). Here, it would be interesting to know what spiritual death is. Those are ailments like sicknesses, pains, frustrations, disappointments, fear, doubts, etc, that are experienced in ones life.

WHY MUST WE CHANGE?

Because of the inherited sin done by Adam and Eve (our first earthly parents), the knowledge of good and bad became known to mankind. Therefore, it is not the wish of God that one should perish; rather, one should have repentance (change) to be able to receive God's glory as promised by Him before the creation of the world. **Please, compare 2nd Peter 3:9.**

From the very beginning, the human heart became adulterated with all kinds of evil – greed, self-righteousness, pride, lies, dishonesty, etc. Prophet Isaiah told us that as we have sinful thoughts so also we have sinful ways of executing them – **Isaiah 55:7.** Because we are individually made with individual destinies, we all react differently to those ailments. One's level of greed differs from another's level of self-righteousness, and so on.

Therefore, be well balanced (temperate, sober of mind), be vigilant and cautious at all times; for that enemy of yours, the devil, roams around like a lion roaring [in fierce hunger], seeking someone to seize upon and devour – 1st Peter 5:8. In the light of these, we should not stop changing from time to time as the devil is a roaring lion looking for whom to consume.

"The devil seeking for whom to devour" means the devil is moving around in spirits, going into man to deposit evil intensions. Therefore, we should test the spirits if they are of God. For the fact that everything belongs to God, does not mean that God would send evil spirits to man. **Please, compare 1st John 4:1; James 1:12-14; Colossians 1:16, 17.** However, God replaced the Spirit He puts in Saul with evil spirit because of his disobedience. **Please, compare 1st Samuel 16:14. Note: The Holy Spirit of God does not delight in rebellion, disobedience, idolatry, or sin of all kinds. Please, compare 1st Samuel 15:23, 24.**

As everyone exercises weaknesses in different dimensions according to human nature, God begins to make us recognize where we are sinning and how we would be reacting to them. **The entrance of the word of God gives light and makes the simple to understand – Psalm 119:130.** As this word pierces our heart, it continues to make the heart diligent. This diligence of the heart is as a result of the word warring against the evil that had been previously (or originally) deposited in our hearts, from the very beginning. **Please, compare Jeremiah 17:9; Proverbs 4:23; Hebrews 4:12.** Moreover, transformation is a process that last one's lifetime. **Please, compare 2nd Peter 3:18.**

HOW TO MAKE GENUINE CHANGE

Prophet Isaiah says, *"Therefore, my people will go into captivity [to their enemies] without knowing it and because they have no knowledge [of God]. And their honourable men [their glory] are famished, and their common people are parched with thirst" – Isaiah 5:13.* Why can't we get this message cleared and followed it as it is written? That is the reason why we all should work diligently towards 'change'.

After the creation of the world, man was called by God to name all other creatures – **Genesis 2:19, 20.** This means that the naming of all other creatures marks the beginning of man's capability to create (as the only creature having the image of God). And when you are creating, you change by shaping and reshaping until it suits the purpose needed. Therefore, it is obligatory that man should continue to change in all ramifications until man becomes what God wants man to be.

The Bible tells us that **every Scripture is God-breathed (given by His inspiration) and profitable for instruction, for reproof and conviction of sin, for correction of error and discipline in obedience, [and] for training in righteousness (in holy living, in conformity to God's will in thought, purpose and action). This will make man to be complete, proficient,** well fitted, and thoroughly equipped for every good work. – 2nd Timothy 3:16, 17.

In this wise, we should seek (aim at and strive after) first of all, His kingdom and His righteousness (His way of doing and being right), and then all these things taken together will be given us besides – Matthew 6:33. Also, Jesus Christ says, *"Not all that say Lord, Lord shall enter into the kingdom of God; but those that obey and do my commands"* – *Matthew 7:21.* Similarly, the philosophers agree that, *"Not everything that glitters is gold."* Therefore, it is our responsibility to find out why it is made so.

Furthermore, as human beings living by purpose, we are 'dynamic' and subject to change at any given time when necessary. Contrarily, as animals that live by instinct, they do as God has programmed into them without changing.

Now, the three major ways we can effect genuine change that will lead us to eternity are:

    (a) Our nature with the Holy Spirit

    (β) Our nature with the world

    (χ) Its application in the world

OUR NATURE WITH THE HOLY SPIRIT

Joshua 1:8 tells us that, "We should not let this Book of the Law depart from our mouth; we should meditate on it day and night, so that we may be careful to do everything written in it. Then, we will be prosperous and successful." I believe this statement needs no further discussion as it is self-explanatory. If we can operate our lives using Bible principles, we would always be on the safe side of winning against the devil.

Moreover, the power of the Holy Spirit was obtained through the death of Jesus Christ on the Cross. Then grace, which is unmerited gift through Christ, was that bestowed righteousness that saved us from the bondage of sins. This is what made us different from the ordinary being. Therefore, we are to use this magnificent potential that has been given to us through the death of Jesus Christ on the Cross of Calvary. **Please, compare Ephesians 2:8, 9.**

Since God is composed of Spirit, there is also a spirit in man through conception. **Please, compare John 4:24; Job 32:8.** As man is the only creature created in the image and likeness of God, His Spirit has to work with the human spirit to develop the character of God in man.

Naturally, all human beings have five main senses. **These are seeing, touching, smelling, hearing, and tasting.** As the human beings now possess godly characters, this spirit (godly) empowers the senses to work with the brain to analyze physical knowledge (godly) and discern its meaning.

To make us have the understanding that genuine change is imminent, the Book of books (Holy Bible) says, *"For the story and message of the cross is sheer absurdity and folly to those who are perishing and on their way to perdition; but to us who are being saved, it is the [manifestation of] the power of God"* – 1st **Corinthians 1:18.**

Additionally, there is now no condemnation (no adjudging guilty of wrong) for those who are in Christ Jesus, who live [and] walk not after the dictates of the flesh, but after the dictates of the Spirit. **Please, compare Romans 8:1; 2nd Corinthians 5:17.**

Here, we should reawaken the dynamism of human beings under two major forces – **godly force and evil force.** I termed them to be **"forces"** because work is being acted on us which invariably moves us from a particular position to another. Actually, these forces are known as godly (Holy Spirit) and Satanic (evil spirits).

The word of God says, *"Beloved, do not put faith in every spirit, but prove (test) the spirits to discover whether they proceed from God; for many false prophets have gone forth into the world" – 1st John 4:1. Also, compare Mark 13:22.* Therefore, to have that **Power** to walk in this dispensation of Christ Jesus, we need to believe the gospel of water and that of the Spirit. **The gospel of water and that of the Spirit are respectively the baptism of Jesus Christ by John the Baptist, and His death on the Cross. Please, compare Matthew 3:15-17; 1st Peter 3:21; John 3:5; Ezekiel 36:25-27.**

Having believed the gospel of water and Spirit, we will now be led by the Holy Spirit; and consequentially, we become sons and daughters of the Most High God – **Romans 8:14.** The Holy Spirit is the power of God at work in our lives. As the Holy Spirit leads us to continue to do and proclaim God's intended purpose in our lives, so also the evil spirits lead those who have already chosen condemnation, to do what is contrary to God's will. **Please, compare John 3:18(b), 19.**

As long as this power from the Father lives in us, it keeps us to be able to have a deep and close relationship with Him. **The Holy Spirit does not drag or push us around; it leads.** This means that the Spirit does not prevent us from sinning or doing otherwise. It only leads us, and we must be ready to follow. **Please, compare Exodus 23:20-22.**

Having known what the Holy Spirit is in the children of God, let us start finding the usefulness of this great-working-power in our lives.

(1) **The Spirit keeps us in close contact with God's mind:** Apostle John says, *"All who keep His commandments [who obey His orders and follows His plan, live and continue to live, to stay and] abide in Him, and He is in them. [They let Christ be a home to them and they are the home of Christ.] And by this, we know and understand and have the proof that He [really] lives and makes His home in us; by the Holy Spirit Whom He has given us" – 1ˢᵗ John 3:24.* By this, God's Spirit works with our minds. Happily enough, our minds are the essential parts of our body that rules our worlds.

(2) **The Holy Spirit helps us come to know His truth:** It is only the truth that will make us free – **John 8:32.** Adding to what we have known, Jesus Christ is the Truth, and He came to deliver the truth. Therefore, if we know Jesus Christ, that is to say, studying Him and how He acted while in flesh, then we know God's truth. **Please, compare John 16:13; 17:17; 14:6; 1:17.**

(3) **The Spirit of God helps us to search and know His word, purpose and will with a deeper understanding: Please, compare 1st Corinthians 2:9-11.** But the natural, non-spiritual man does not accept or welcome or admit into his heart the gifts and teachings and revelations of the Spirit of God, for they are folly (meaningless nonsense) to him; and he is incapable of knowing them (of progressively recognizing, understanding, and becoming better acquainted with them) because they are spiritually discerned and estimated and appreciated – **1st Corinthians 2:14.**

(4) **It makes the impossible to be possible: Romans 8:26 says, "So too the [Holy] Spirit comes to our aid and bears us up in our weaknesses; for we do not know what prayer to offer nor how to offer it worthily as we ought, but the Spirit Himself goes to meet our supplication and pleads in our behalf with unspeakable yearnings and groanings too deep for utterance."** Yes, I can do all things through Christ that strengthens me – **Philippians 4:13.**

God does not want us to be the same way we have been before He called us – **Romans 12:2.** Therefore, as we transform by the entire renewal of our minds, the Holy Spirit now help us to have the same attitude, purpose, and (humble) mind of Christ. Yes, what can separate us from the love of God if the Holy Spirit dwells in us? Joyfully enough, with God, all things are possible. Please, compare **Philippians 2:5; Romans 8:37-39; Matthew 19:26; Mark 10:27.**

(5) **The Spirit helps us to see sin as it really is:** From this very moment, our bodies have now become the temple of God. Consequently, it should not be defiled. As we continue to keep the Spirit within us consecrated, He helps us to recognize and avoid sin. **Please, compare 1st Corinthians 3:16; John 16:8.**

(6) **The Spirit produces godly fruits in us:** Every tree shall bear the fruit of its kind – **Genesis 1:12.** Likewise, God Spirit produces godly fruits – love, joy (gladness), peace, patience (an even temper, forbearance), kindness, goodness (benevolence), faithfulness, gentleness (meekness, humility), self-control (self-restraint, continence). Against such things, there is no law [that can bring a charge]. **Please, compare Galatians 5:22, 23.**

As we know Christ, His divine power [Holy] Spirit has given us everything we need for life. Through the promises bestowed upon us, we may escape the moral decadence and corruption in the world. On this note, strive to make sure that your calling and election is real, virile and solicitous; so that you will never stumble and fall. In the end, you will receive a rich welcome into the eternal kingdom of our Lord and Saviour Jesus Christ. **Please, compare 2nd Peter 1:3-11.**

(7) **The Spirit of God acts as a Comforter in our lives:** When we say comforter, we mean as a friend going side-by-side with us as a helper. Therefore, we should not be dismayed or discouraged over any situation as everything will work together for good for those that **love Christ**

according to His will and purpose. **Please, compare John 14:16, 17, 26; Romans 8:28.**

Working with these principles, our nature with the Spirit would be corrected; and we can walk with God to the place He had prepared for those who are called to be His own. **Please, compare Exodus 23:20-22; 19:5**

In the light of these, Jesus says*, "It is the Spirit Who gives life [He is the Life-giver]; the flesh conveys no benefit whatever [there is no profit in it]. The words (truths) that I have been speaking to you are spirit and life"* – John 6:63.

OUR NATURE WITH THE WORLD

Interestingly, as followers of Christ and born-again children [i.e., changed from the way of the world (fleshly) to the way of Christ (spiritually)], we are aware of the opposing spirits, otherwise known as 'evil spirits'. And the producer of these spirits is Satan the Devil.

Also, we are happy to know how Satan came into this sinful world according to the Book of the Law. In the Bible, we are told that he is a roaring lion, thief, destroyer and killer who came to steal our joy. Agreed! Now, the question before us is, how does he operates?

Dear readers, here is the most sensitive part where we have to pay more attention! The devil is not living in my house, your office; neither is he coming from Africa. The spirits (evil spirits) he produces are invited into our lives individually. The process is like a person living in his apartment under closed doors. When another person (known or unknown) knocks, the coming in of the purported visitor depends on the owner of the apartment. If he opens the door, the visitor is welcomed. On the contrary, if he refuses (no matter what it takes), the person cannot force his/her way in. That is how the devil comes into our lives through our minds. Remember, it is your mind that creates your world. However, **"Satan – Our Only Enemy is dealt with in Chapter Three.**

The acceptance of Satan's words to Eve as being like God, to know what is good and bad was what led to the eating of the forbidden fruit. That is to say, they (Eve and Adam) have allowed the devil to enter into their minds by believing the lie told by Satan. **Please, compare Genesis Chapter 3; Luke 22:3.** Measurably, this act of disobedience carries a penalty punishable by death.

This death, like most people believe, is to live in anyway we can; and when a time comes, we would die (physical death). In reality, it is not only that; also is the spiritual death, where we have feelings of uncertainties, fear, having pains (directly or indirectly), suffering from outrageous maladies, disappointments, hindrances, etc.

Because God is love and loved man even before his creation, His being jealous over the breach of covenant made Him to bring in a sinless Being to take away all these reproach by sharing His blood on the Cross of Calvary. **Oh Jesus Christ – the 'One and Only' immeasurable friend to mankind. How wonderful is your holy name!**
Have we ever looked critically into the Ten Laws of Prophet Moses **(Exodus.20:1-21), and asked ourselves if we are following them?** Those Laws were combined together and made two by our Saviour Jesus Christ.

Luke10:27 tells us that, "Love the Lord your God with all your heart, soul, strength, and mind; and 'Love your neighbour as yourself'." He further advised us, "If we refuse to do this, we are not doing His work." Also, compare Leviticus 19:18, and Deuteronomy 6:5.

The Bible says, *"Thou shall not judge others so that we may not be judged" – Matthew 7:1, 2.* Since we cannot judge, however, we have the power to sense and suggest correction **(Ephesians 5:11-14).** How many of us on earth today are obeying those Laws of Jesus Christ? That is to say, **just love one and another** as God loves you. Fortunately, when you know what love is, and you extend it to your neighbour, nothing will make you harm your neighbour. However, you cannot give what you don't have.

Here, God made it clear to us that we shall reap what we sow. Therefore, as Christians (who have faith in God through Christ), we are supposed to put on the full armour of God to show examples worthy of emulation.

Vividly, The Parable of the Good Samaritan has explained this. **Please, read Luke 10:25-37.** We should show love to be a rational decision to secure the highest good, personally whenever need and opportunity were present, to anyone without prejudices, in spite of fear; and to follow through logically and responsibly even if it should mean personal cost.

At this juncture, a question may arise, **'Who is my neighbour?'** Nevertheless, it would have been better put, **'To whom can I be a neighbour?'** Moreover, legalism looks for limits; love looks for opportunities. As selfishness finds every possible excuse, love finds a way past all obstacles. Therefore, it is indispensable for us to know that love covers a multitude of sins.

According to the Bible, it is possible to give all our goods to feed the poor, and still not have love. **Love is patient, love is kind. It does not envy, it does not boast, it is not proud. It is not rude, it is not self-seeking, it is not easily angered, and it keeps no record of wrongs. Love does not delight in evil, but rejoices with the truth. It always protects, trusts, hopes, and perseveres – 1st Corinthians 13:3-7.** Remember, this is God's kind of love for us and is unconditional.

In fact, there is no true religion apart from true morality, and there is no true morality apart from love. Without love, there is no holiness.

What is more, as Jesus was teaching His disciples on how they should pray (i.e., Our Lord's Prayer), He said, *"Forgive us our debts, as we also have forgiven (left, remitted, and let go of the debts, and have given up resentment against) our debtors" – Matthew 6:12.* As Christians, we keep resentments on people for what they have done unto us. How do we expect Our Father to forgive us our transgressions when we refuse to forgive others?

Emphatically, I am stating here that we should love our enemies so that our blessings would be full. Though, people might say, 'It is easier said than done.' Truly, it is what is expected of us as the chosen ones of Our Father who hath in Heaven. **Therefore, Romans 12:21 is advising us to overcome evil with good. Please, don't forget! As Christians, the Conqueror and Master told us to be wise as serpents and harmless as doves – Matthew 10:16.**

IT'S APPLICATION IN THE WORLD

Individually, we all have ideas of what we have to change. Because we are living in the present situation, how do we relate this issue to this sinful world? Let us remember *Romans 12:2 again: "Do not be conformed to this world (this age), [fashioned after and adapted to its external, superficial customs], but be transformed (changed) by the [entire] renewal of your mind [by its new ideals and its new attitude], so that you may prove [for yourselves] what is the good, acceptable, and perfect will of God, even the thing which is good, acceptable, and perfect [in His sight for you].*

This therefore, takes us to the ways people think about **'change.'** However, as we know that, we will then suggest the ways **'change'** should be in order to enhance profitable living.

To begin with, most people change just to get away from their problem. Unfortunately, such **'change'** is not enough to solve the supposed-problem. This situation is like painting a rusty surface without first 'sand-papering' that surface. When dried, the paint can wear off, then bringing the surface to a worsened state.

Changing your circumstances to improve your life is temporary. It can re-surface. **It is better and almost permanent to 'change' ourselves to improve our circumstances.** Please, don't forget! People do what people see. Today, imitation and modeling are becoming human priorities. Learn to imitate what is morally inclined as your blessings would be full, on the long run.

Here, it pertinent to know that you don't have the power to change yourself! It is He who made heavens and earth that can change you. He can harden your heart as you refuse to change when you were supposed to; and He can have mercy on those He wants to have mercy on. He does everything according to His will and purpose. Therefore, it is worthwhile you make move towards repentance so as His grace would manifest. Please, compare 2nd Corinthians 12:9; Romans 2:4; 9:13-16; Exodus 7:3; Luke 22:42; Matthew 6:10.

Remember, you cannot sow rice and reap potatoes. Doing the same thing, same time, all day, would always produce same results. When you want something to change, you should involve in something you've never done. Consequently, you would expect a new outcome, in the light of these.

We should learn to change when we see the '**light**'. This would make the change almost permanent. **When we wait until we feel the 'heat', the changing might become difficult and almost impossible.** Here, we should remember a Senior Statesman – Late Obafemi Awolowo. In one of his political campaign tours, in Nigeria, he said, **"When peaceful change becomes impossible, violent change becomes inevitable." Yes, we have to make hay while the sun shines!**

Another reason why most people refuse to change is because of the unwillingness to pay the immediate price. For instance, a smoker or prostitute may find it difficult to change that habit because of the joy he/she derives from it. However, if any decides to change it for other things having moral inclination, he/she would receive the rewards in full, and it would be permanent. To buttress that, as Christ performed His healing power on those held in captivity, He made the injunction: *"Sin no more."*

Finally, most people see change as **'hurtful'**, instead of seeing it as **'helpful'**. Agreed! It may be hurtful and difficult as one is changing from a known activity to a new and unfamiliar activity. Nevertheless, change (morally) is helpful as it takes us to a new activity, according to the will and purpose of God. For with God, nothing is ever impossible; and no word from God shall be without power or impossible of fulfillment. **Please, compare Luke 1:37.**

In general, we are living directly or indirectly in a painful world. You and I cannot eradicate it. Therefore, now is the time of rededication. A time to reiterate the Word, and 'be soaked' in Him.

Jesus Christ is above all our circumstances. As our steps are being ordered by God, we have to walk and be in Spirit always. We should not allow our circumstances to overtake our visions. Otherwise, we would be people of unfulfilled visions. **Please, compare John 3:31; Psalm 37:23.**

Moreover, there is a Chinese saying, **"When righteousness climbs a meter, the devil climbs ten meters."** This means that the devil always try to conquer righteousness. In the same way, the same people still believe that, **"When the Way grows, the devil disappears"**, which explains that the Way and devil can never exist together. **Please, compare Galatians 5:17.**

Above all, we should learn not to compromise and fall into slavery; for Jesus has come to set us free from slavery of all kinds – **Galatians 5:1.**

Naturally, the green mountains are motionless; the white clouds come and go by themselves. If we are not

transformed by our environment, we will transform it. If we are not transformed by the devil, we can overcome him.

Summing it up, there is nothing to fear except fear. Remember, the reverent and worshipful fear of the Lord is the beginning, principal and choice part of knowledge [its starting point and its essence]; but fools despise skillful and godly Wisdom, instruction, and discipline. **Please, compare Proverbs 1:7; Psalm 111:10.**

Therefore, Apostle Paul ascertains that: *"If any person is [in-grafted] in Christ (the Messiah) he is a new creation (a new creature altogether); the old [previous moral and spiritual condition] has passed away. Behold, the fresh and new has come"* – 2nd *Corinthians 5:17.*

Again, let me reaffirm and buttress the point: Only God has the power to change anybody! He has made the world by Himself and for Himself. He can harden your heart as you refuse to change when you were supposed to; and He can have mercy on those He wants to have mercy on. He does everything according to His will and purpose. Again and with more emphasis, it is worthwhile you make move towards repentance so as His grace would manifest in your life. Please, compare Colossians 1:16, 17; Deuteronomy 30:19; 2nd Corinthians 12:9; Romans 9:13-16; Exodus 7:3; Luke 22:42; Matthew 6:10; 2nd Peter 3:9.

Since we have known that human beings are dynamic and subject to change at any point in time, let us now find out how we could use **Prayer** as the instrument needed to bring heavens down to earth, as we **Walk In The Light** that has no shadow of turning.

CHAPTER TWO

THE EFFICACY OF PRAYER

"Elijah was a human being with a nature such as we have [with feelings, affections, and a constitution like ours]; and he prayed earnestly for it not to rain, and no rain fell on earth for three years and six months. And [then] he prayed again and the heavens supplied rain and the land produced its crops [as usual]" – James 5:17, 18. Yes, the prayer of a righteous man avails much.

"You know the value of prayer; it is precious beyond all prices. Never, never neglect it" – Sir Thomas Buxton.

"I beseech You, O Lord, [earnestly] remember now how I have walked before You in faithfulness and truth and with a whole heart [entirely devoted to You] and have done what is good in Your sight. And Hezekiah wept bitterly. Turn back and tell Hezekiah, the leader of My people. Thus says the Lord, the God of David your [forefather]: I have heard your prayer, I have seen your tears; and behold, I will heal you. On the third day you shall go up to the house of the Lord" – 2nd Kings 20:3, 5.

"By the word of the Lord were the heavens made, and all their host by the breath of His mouth" – Psalms 33:6.

"Death and life are in the power of the tongue, and they who indulge in it shall eat the fruit of it [for death or life] – Proverbs 18:21.

The angel of the Lord appeared to Daniel saying, "Fear not Daniel, for from the first day you set your mind and heart to understand and humble yourself before your God, your words were heard, and I have come as a consequence of [and in response to] your words" – **Daniel 10:12.**

On the Cross, before His last breath, Jesus prayed the Father to forgive His conspirators as they do not know what they were doing. Jesus started with prayer and ended with prayer. After His baptism, He was led into the wilderness by the Holy Spirit. In the wilderness, He fasted for forty days and nights. After this divine exercise, He was tempted by the devil. And, He was able to overcome the plots of the devil with the help of the **Anointing Spirit** in Him.

WHAT IS PRAYER?

This is the act of communicating with a deity (especially as a petition, or in adoration, or contrition, or thanksgiving). **For the purpose of this message, it is the reverent petition to God, the Creator of heavens and earth.** Prayer runs parallel with the will of God, as He will have all men to be saved and to come unto the knowledge of truth. Prayer reaches up to heaven, and brings heaven down to earth. **Please, compare 1st Timothy 2:1-4.**

ESSENTIALS OF PRAYER

God, in His supernatural love, created us in His image. Undoubtedly, He had prepared the best for us. **Please, compare Exodus 23:20; Jeremiah 29:11.** It is in Him that we should have the best in our existence. However, the antagonist is moving to and fro to sway, or divert that bestowed blessing. The Divine Teacher (Holy Bible) teaches us that God formed the light and created darkness. He brings prosperity and also creates disaster – **Isaiah 45:7.** Therefore, for us to be on the safe-positive-side (blessings), we need to pray (ask in the name of Christ Jesus) to have the blessings, and against the enemy.

Prayer, to a believer is like a cutlass to a farmer; also, like a pen and paper to a writer. A farmer may go to the farm without cutlass; nevertheless, he might be able to do certain work like removing the soft weeds with his fingers. On the other hand, he needs the cutlass to cut down the trees and other obstacles. In fact, today, he needs more sophisticated machineries to pull down these obstacles.

The only supernatural machinery that can pull down all obstacles is by requesting from God with humility. All insurmountable mountains will be brought to level grounds when you let God know in prayer. **Don't forget! If you do not ask, you may not be given.**

After the resurrection of Christ Jesus, He said that all authority in heavens and on earth has been given to Him – **Matthew 28:18.** Therefore, anything we need, we should ask in prayer, thanksgiving and supplication – **Philippians 4:6.** Additionally, we should not stop asking from God until we are established – **Isaiah 62:6, 7.**

Sometimes, the question comes to mind: "**Does God answers all prayers?**" In His ability, He created the world by Himself and for Himself – **Colossians 1:16, 17.** Everything (including man) is created for His will, glory and purpose – **Isaiah 43:7.** Therefore, He answers all prayers in His capability and way He desires. **Please, read 1ˢᵗ Peter 3:10-12; Psalms 10:4; Romans 12:19-21.**

In the light of these, we are exhorted to be diligent and faithful in prayer since it is our access to God for a life of spiritual intimacy, and is the means by which God advances His kingdom. **Please, compare Romans 12:12.**

HAVING AN EFFECTIVE PRAYER

Before we pray, we have to open our hearts and close our minds. No man with narrow views of God, of His great plan to save men, and of the universal needs of all men, can pray effectually. **It takes a broad-minded man, who understands God and His purposes in the atonement, to pray well.** An effectual prayer comes from a big heart, filled with thoughts about all men and with sympathies for all men.

As the whole nature of man enters into prayer, so also all that belongs to man is the beneficiary of prayer. In addition, when praying to God, we have to be sincere with reverence and godly fear. *Hebrews 10:22 says, "Let us all come forward and draw near with true (honest and sincere) hearts in unqualified assurance and absolute conviction engendered by faith (by that leaning of the entire human personality on God in absolute trust and confidence in His power, wisdom and goodness), having our hearts sprinkled and purified from guilty (evil) conscience and our bodies cleansed with pure water."*

Since God is responsible and permits all (good and bad), and also our greatest Provider; therefore, we should ask for anything we need, in His name (Jesus Christ) and through prayer. Unfortunately enough, we have never asked – **John 16:23, 24.** While asking, we should remain faithful and have full belief that it will be done according to our heart desire. **Please, compare John 15:7; Matthew 7:7, 8; Matthew 21:21, 22; Psalm 106:15; Numbers 14:28.**

Furthermore, to have an effective prayer, we must humble ourselves by keeping our minds out of worry and anxiety. As we continue to thank God with humility, loving one and another, we will be receiving what we have requested for in prayer. **Please, compare Philippians 4:6; Galatians 5:6.**

TYPES OF PRAYER

There are three main kinds of prayer made known to us in the Scripture. They are Secret Prayer, Intercessory Prayer, and The Lord's Prayer.

(a) <u>**Secret Prayer:**</u>
Secret prayer is the kind of prayer made in secret to our Father who hears in secret, and rewards us in the open – **Matthew 6:6; 1st Samuel 1:9-17.** A private place is a place of quiet and calm, where the believer enjoys meeting his heavenly Father. The light which shines there is a life-giving light; and the inspiring atmosphere which fill it, is the breath of the Holy Spirit. This is the breath that pours

God's love into the heart. When you pray, try not to make repetition of words as the Father knows your heart before you ask Him. **Please, compare Matthew 6:7, 8.**

Furthermore, when the Great Teacher said: **"Pray to your Father who is in secret"**, He wanted us to understand that God is not seen by the physical eye; rather, by the eye of the day. His light shines in the heart of every worshipper who detaches himself from the world, surrenders to the leadership of the Spirit of Christ, Who brings him into the very presence of God. **Please, compare John 14:17; 16:13; 17:17.**

The secret place, the shut door, and detachment from things around us, are only a means to prepare a quiet and holy sanctuary that we can meditate deeply on the profession of God and His love which takes the role of Fatherhood.

Furthermore, we should bear in our hearts that being behind closed doors does not make us alone in the room. The Almighty Father is with us wherever we are. Moreover, Jesus Christ was always going away from the disciples to a solitary place, like on top of the mountain to pray – **Matthew 14:23; Mark 1:35; Luke 4:42; 5:16.** Yes, He was always having a direct communication with the Father. **Please, compare Isaiah 43:2.**

(b)   Intercessory Prayer:
Intercessory prayer is the kind of prayer where a man of God has to be between God, and who is being prayed for. **Please, compare Job 42:8.** This is the kind of prayer mostly performed by church leaders. More interestingly, the preacher is to lay himself out in prayer for his people; not that they might be saved, simply; but that they will be mightily saved. **Please, read 1st Timothy 2:1-5.**

(c) **The Lord's Prayer:**

The third kind of prayer is **"The Lord's Prayer."** This is the prayer which seems to be universal in nature. When the disciples asked Jesus to teach them how to pray, the Son of Man thought them The Lord's Prayer – **Matthew 6:9-13.**

In **Matthew 6:11,** we ask God to give us today our daily bread. This is the need of the body; and it would help us to carry out our daily spiritual duties. We should be faithful to this prayer and believe that the God that has made us to see today, through grace, would satisfy our needs according to His riches, glory in Christ Jesus, will and purpose.

More so, we should not behave like the (then) Israelites, who, when freed from Egypt fretted that they have nothing to eat in the wilderness as was in Egypt. Then, God spoke to Moses that He will give them food. All they have to do is to take what is necessary for a day, just to test how they will be loyal to His commandment – **Exodus 16:3, 4.**

However, they heard what Moses said to them, but never did according to how God commanded them. Instead, they gathered more than they can eat for a day. Later, the remnants became worms as they were preserved to the next day. **Please, read Exodus Chapter 16.**

As children created by God in His image, we are obliged to obey His commandments. If we ask for what we need daily to walk with God, we will be given. And, the blessing we will be given would give a continuous day-to-day unending joy, peace, fulfillment, etc. Therefore, let us always change the thoughts in our hearts before we make our request, petition unto God. **Please, compare 1st Peter 3:10-12.**

Matthew 6:12 says, "Forgive us our debts, as we also have forgiven our debtors." Here, Jesus is talking about forgiveness in general. He sees it as one of the stumbling blocks (sins) that would hinder our prayer before God. If we do not forgive others who has trespassed against us, our Father would also not forgive us our trespasses against others and Himself. Nevertheless, our God is a merciful Father who gives us time to repent. Thus, He is slow to anger; but full of compassion. **Please, compare Psalm 145:8.**

"Lead us not into temptation, but deliver us from the evil one." We were told in the Gospel of Saint Mark that after His baptism, the Holy Spirit led Jesus into the wilderness to fast for forty days and nights. Immediately after this incident, He was tempted by the devil. Actually, God can never be tempted, neither does He tempts anyone. Humans are being carried away by their own evil desires, lust and passion. **Please, compare James 1:13, 14.**

In essence, what really happened here was that Jesus Christ, being in human flesh has to show us what we are to pass through in this evil-angry world. As long as He has come to fulfil the Law, He came through temptation (moral decadence) and succeeded it. Equally, we are to pass through temptations, but overcome them following Jesus Christ wisdom. Please, don't forget! "Falling into temptation is doing what is expected to be avoided." Please, compare Matthew 5:17.

Nevertheless, there are times we might be tested of our faith; and these times, we should pray that we should be able to overcome. We knew what happened during the **'time of storm' with Jesus and His disciples – Matthew 8:23-27.** With prayers, the wind was rebuked and became calm. *"You men of little faith, why are you afraid?"* Today, this situation is affecting most believers or born-again Christians – that is to say, the ability of relying fully on what we know, and not fully putting our confidence in God. **Please, compare Proverbs 3:5-7.**

Therefore, having trials and tribulations are joyful exercises permitted by God. Our own side is to pray over them as the Master whom we are following has overcome. Jesus began with prayer and ended with prayer – **Matthew 26:36-44.**

As He was praying, He began to know what is coming ahead of Him. Then, He became depressed and distressed and said, ***"My Father, if it is possible, let this cup pass away from Me; nevertheless, not what I will [not what I desire], but as You will and desire" Matthew 26:39.*** On the Cross of Calvary, Jesus prayed for us all to be forgiven as we did not know what we were doing. **Please, compare James 1:12; John 16:33; Luke 23:34.**

Over-emphasizing the issue of trials and tribulations, Jesus instructed His disciples: ***"All of you must keep awake (give strict attention, be cautious and active) and watch and pray that you may not come into temptation. The spirit indeed is willing, but the flesh is weak" – Matthew 26:41.*** More so, though, He was tempted by the devil, He was able to overcome Satan's craftiness through the Holy Spirit in Him and fervent prayer.

Now is the time for the church leaders to be more dedicated to prayer like the yesteryear apostles. This will help eradicate the sad, dark times of today's worldliness. ***James 5:14 says, "Is anyone of you sick? He should call the elders of the church to pray over him and anoint him with oil in the name of our Lord Jesus Christ."* PLEASE**

NOTE: Sickness in this respect is not only physical sickness. Also, it includes spiritual sicknesses like weakness in faith and in praying, financial backwardness, ignorance, lack of wisdom, etc.

Therefore, for us to enter into God's kingdom, we must fervently pray with a keen understanding of "Our Lord's Prayer." In reality, God's kingdom is the government of Christ that is to come and destroy this present evil age ruled by Satan the Devil. However, in this context, God's kingdom is making yourself a holy sanctuary by repenting of your evil deeds, abiding in Jesus Christ, and obeying His message!

In the light of these, God will now start dwelling in you, in the form of the Holy Spirit, giving you the power to destroy all works of evil. Please, compare Matthew 6:33; Mark 1:15; John 14:23; Philippians 2:12, 13; 3:13, 14. Happily enough, in God's kingdom, there is power, liberty, accomplishments, successes, overcoming, etc.

BENEFITS OF PRAYER

Prayer has in its hands a double blessing. It rewards him who prays, and blesses him who is prayed for. It brings peace to warring passions and calms warring elements. Tranquility is the happy fruit of true praying. Prayer creates quiet and peaceable lives in all godliness and honesty.

Now, we have known the significance of prayer to mankind. Therefore, prayer is universal in its application to all men and to all subjects. This makes prayer to be made everywhere in the world. ***In 1ˢᵗ Timothy 2:1-3, Paul says, "First of all, then, I admonish and urge that petitions, prayers, intercessions, and thanksgivings be offered on behalf of all men, for kings and all those in authority, that we may live peaceful and quiet lives in all godliness and holiness. This is good and pleases God our Saviour."***

Consequently, leaders are to be prayed for; because, they are not out of the reach and control of prayer, as they are not out of the reach and control of God. The time Apostle Paul made this comment, the king of the Romans then was Nero. History says that he was wicked to mankind.

Church leaders and state rulers need prayer; because, prayer makes mighty potencies. It makes them better rulers and restrains their lawlessness and autocratic mindfulness. Right praying not only makes life beautiful in peace, but redolent in righteousness and weighty in influence. Honesty, gravity, integrity, and weight in character are the natural and essential fruits of prayer.

It is practically known that in solving any mathematical problem, the formulae are needed. Having known the formulae, just fix in the figures and we are done. Similarly, as believers (in God through Christ Jesus), the only problem we have on our way to eternity is Satan. Now that we know the power of prayer before Satan; that is to say, one of the major weapons against his schemes, we have to use it to claim the joy our Father gave to us through our Lord Jesus Christ, and even before the world began.

2ⁿᵈ Corinthians 10:3-5 say, "For though we walk (live) in the flesh, we are not carrying on our warfare according to the flesh and using mere human weapons.

For the weapons of our warfare are not physical [weapons of flesh and blood], but they are mighty before God for the overthrow and destruction of strongholds. [Inasmuch as we] refute arguments and theories and reasonings and every proud and lofty thing that sets itself up against the [true] knowledge of God; and we lead every thought and purpose away captive into the obedience of Christ (the Messiah, the Anointed One)." Therefore, we must pray endlessly for divine favour and fulfilment. This is one of the ways to put on the whole armour of God; because, we are fighting against principalities, powers of darkness and even in high places.

Emphatically, therefore, it is by prayer only that all things are delivered to us by the Father through the Son. Also, it is only by prayer that all things are revealed to us by the Father and by the Son. And, most importantly, of all things done to man by God, is by revealing Himself to man; and this is done only by prayer.

Prayer is one of the eminent characteristics of strong spiritual leadership. Men of mighty prayer are men of might and mold things. Their power with God has the conquering tread.

Jesus has reliably informed us that many of us will be persecuted in His name; and when it happens, we should not fear, for He has overcome. Now, Paul and Silas were put into prison for casting out the evil spirit in the slave girl. When midnight came, they went into fervent prayer. The impact of this prayer was so tremendous that the prison attendant became converted immediately, as he and his family could not resist standing on the opposing side of God. **Please, compare 2nd Timothy 3:12; Acts 16:25, 26.**

Therefore, Apostle Paul proclaimed, **"Giving ourselves continually to prayer is the consensus of apostolic devotion."**

Also, Daniel was finding favour from King Darius as the power of God made him to distinguish himself among the administrators of the land. His comrades hated him and persuaded the king to enact a law that would deny all inhabitants from praying to any other god (or God) except King Darius.

Daniel, who loved his God more than ever, refused to obey that law, and performed his usual three-times prayer to God each day. However, this time, it is done at the upstairs room where the windows are opened towards Jerusalem. In that light, he was thrown into lions' den. God, knowing fully well that His servant is being punished for His sake, has to shut the mouths of the lions and they became harmless. **This is the Supremacy of Christ. Please, read Colossians 1:16, 17.**

As the king saw that Daniel was not embarrassed by the lions, then, he tested the action of the lions by using the perpetrators of Daniel. Immediately the gates were shut against these men, the lions attacked them; and not even a piece of their bones was left. Everything was eaten up by the hungry lions. Therefore, King Darius enacts another decree for all inhabitants of the land to serve the God of Daniel as that is the living God. **Please, read Daniel Chapter 6.**

A non-praying Christian will never know God's truth; and he will remain a powerless believer. Owing to this view, pray without ceasing is the trumpet-call of the missionary leaders of the 21st century – **1st Thessalonians 5:16-18.** To the best of it all, prayer became the bridge through which panic runs into peace, in the light of these.

WAYS OF PRAYING

Praying can be done by standing, kneeling, spreading out hands, and bowing. Sometimes, we can pray by prostrating. Though, there is no stipulated or steadfast manner (position) on praying recorded in the Scriptures; however, Jesus displayed a pattern by throwing Himself upon the ground on His face – **Matthew 26:39.**

In the conversation with a Samaritan Woman, Jesus said: *"The heavenly Father seeks worshippers, and it pleases Him when we worship Him. In this wise, it would be most proper to worship Him in Truth and in Spirit; because, God is Spirit. Therefore, we should always pray in Spirit so that the Father can receive us in Spirit" – John 4:23, 24.* Consequently, in the course of worshipping God, it would be more appropriate to put down our knees while praying. It denotes the exhibition of humility.

IMPORTANCE OF PRAYER

Encouraging us on the importance of prayer to mankind, our Father empowers the Holy Spirit to help intercede for us even if we do not know what to pray for. *"In the same way, the Spirit helps us in our weakness. We do not know what we ought to pray for, but the Spirit Himself intercedes for us with groans that words cannot express" – Romans 8:26.*

Jesus started with prayer and ended with prayer. Prayer is universal to all men, all things, all situations, and in all places. ***Philippians 4:19 says, "My God will liberally supply (fill to the full) our every need according to His riches in glory in Christ Jesus."*** Therefore, praying with faith and belief will make a way for God to work for us where there seems to be no way. **Please, compare James 1:5-8.**

Educating us more on the importance of prayer, ***Prophet Isaiah lectures: "Our God have posted watchmen on the walls of Jerusalem; they will never be silent day or night. We who call on the Lord should give ourselves no rest, and give Him (God) also no rest until He establishes us and makes us the praise of the earth" – Isaiah 62:6, 7.***

Finally, therefore, ***God gave us this instruction: "If My people who are called by My name, shall humble themselves, pray, seek, crave, and require of necessity My face and turn from their wicked ways, then will I hear from heaven, forgive their sin, and heal their land" – 2nd Chronicles 7:14.***

CONCLUSION

In conclusion, prayer is the master key that unlocks the sealed doors of all blessings. On the other hand, it is the greatest weapon that breaks all demonic rocks into pieces, thereby bringing all supposed-insurmountable mountains to level grounds.

Now that we have got the weapon that destroys all strongholds (calamity, disappointments, hatred, pains, etc.), let us progress in the direction of our goal by knowing who Satan is, and plots to destroy his schemes.

CHAPTER THREE

SATAN – OUR ONLY ENEMY

The Holy Bible says, "Put on God's whole armour [the armour of a heavy-armed soldier which God supplies], that you may be able successfully to stand up against [all] the strategies and the deceits of the devil. Know it, we are not wrestling with flesh and blood [contending only with physical opponents], but against the despotisms, against the powers, [the master spirits who are] the world rulers of this present darkness, against the spirit forces of wickedness in the heavenly (supernatural) sphere. Therefore, put on God's complete armour, that you may be able to resist and stand your ground on the evil day [of danger], and having done all [the crisis demands], to stand [firmly in your place]. Stand therefore [hold your ground], having tightened the belt of truth around your loins and having put on the breastplate of integrity, and of moral rectitude and right standing with God" – Ephesians 6:11-14.

"Though we walk (live) in the flesh, we are not carrying on our warfare according to the flesh and using mere human weapons. For the weapons of our warfare are not physical [weapons of flesh and blood], but they are mighty before God for the overthrow and destruction of strongholds. [Inasmuch as we] refute arguments, theories, reasoning, and every proud and lofty thing that sets itself up against the [true] knowledge of God; and we lead every thought and purpose away captive into the

obedience of Christ (the Messiah, the Anointed One)" – 2nd Corinthians 10:3-5.

Furthermore, the thief (devil) comes only in order to steal, kill and destroy. Jesus Christ came that we may have and enjoy life, and have it in abundance (to the full, till it overflows) – John 10:10.

DOES SATAN REALLY EXIST?

It has come to the notice of many, that just as most people do not believe in the existence of a Creator (God), also, they do not have the awareness of the existence of Satan the Devil. Most people believe that if there is the knowledge of Satan in this world, it means there is no God. On the other hand, if there is a Creator that controls heavens and earth, it means that He is not powerful enough to rule the world.

Though, psychological however, if we have knowledge or in search of knowledge, we would know more about ourselves and the world we are living in.

Searching the Scripture, we have been able to know that before the creation of man, spirit creatures have already been in existence. Compare Job 38:4, 7; John 1:1-5. Because God is a Spirit, no human eye has ever seen Him – John 4:24. In the same vein, other spirit beings, which existed before man's creation, are never seen by the naked eye. They are God's messengers known as angels. Please, compare Hebrews 1:13, 14.

One of the angels noticed that man being created in the image of God, and made to multiply would have to live spiritually for God. **Please, compare Isaiah 43:7.** Because of greed and enviousness, the angel 'opposed' God; by going into the serpent to deceive the woman. Remember, as an angel who carries God's message, he has the foresight of knowing man more than man knows himself. He knew the woman to be the weaker vessel; thus, he used her to achieve his selfish ends. **Please, compare 1st Peter 3:7.**

Firstly, Eve objected to the plot of the serpent by saying, *"If we eat from the fruit, we would die."* Then, the serpent 'pressed' further to say, *"You positively would not die. You will only be like God knowing what is good and bad." Please, read Genesis 3:1-5.*

Commenting on that fateful conversation, Mary Baker Eddy, in her book, **Science and Health with Keys to Scriptures, ascertains:** *"Physiology is one of the apples from 'the tree of knowledge.' Evil declared that eating this fruit would open man's eyes and make him as God. Instead of so doing, it closed the eyes of mortals to man's God-given dominion over the earth."*

Since this lie was told by this angel in order to have his heart desire, therefore, he is a slanderer called Devil. And being an adversary to God because he wants man to worship him instead of God, he is then known as Satan. This is where the angel (**Lucifer, the bright and morning star**) who was once a right-hand-creature of God earns the name **"Satan the Devil."**

Over-emphasizing the presence of evil spirits in the world, the Book of Saint Mark has this to say. A man possessed by demon could not be stopped or calmed by anyone. He broke loose of the chains and was disturbing the peace of the environment. Nevertheless, as he saw Jesus, he bowed down and negotiated with Him on how he should be treated. **Please, read Mark 5:1-20.**

Furthermore, the Bible tells us that there was war in heaven between God's angels and that of the dragon. And the gigantic dragon was cast down and sent out of heaven. He was flung out alongside with his angels down to earth. **Please, read Revelation Chapter 12.**

Also, the Bible was able to enlighten us that the world is not fighting against flesh and blood, but against the despotisms, against the powers, [the master spirits who are] the world rulers of this present darkness, against the spirit forces of wickedness in the heavenly (supernatural) places. Please, read Ephesians 6:11, 12.

Now, it is vividly clear to us that there is the presence of the evil spirits moving in the world. And the aim of Satan on earth is to deny us of the endless joy God has pre-planned for us before we were created – **John 10:10.** Also compare **Revelations 12:10, 13, and 17.** In this light, *2nd Corinthians 4:4 says, "The god of this world has blinded the unbelievers' minds [that they should not discern the truth], preventing them from seeing the illuminating light of the Gospel of the glory of Christ (the Messiah), Who is the image and Likeness of God."*

HOW HE (SATAN) OPERATES

Since the devil has exercised unseen influence over human affairs, he has been able to turn people away from worshipping the true God; and simultaneously bowing down to him (Satan). **We can see that in the temptation of Christ in Matthew 4:8, 9. Yes, this angel is moving** about in spirit like a roaring lion seeking for whom to devour – 1ˢᵗ Peter 5:8.

As people were using the name of our Lord Jesus Christ in vain to challenge the devil's scheme, the devil replied by saying: *"Jesus I know, and Paul I know about. But, who are you?"* To confirm his power over those who are spiritually dead, the Bible tells us that the man in whom the evil spirit dwelt leaped upon them, mastering two of them, and was so violent against them that they dashed out of that house [in fear], stripped naked and wounded. **Please, read Acts 19:13-16.**

In reality, everybody has been given potentials –human spirit (which is later replaced with the Holy Spirit having followed the ordinances of God), talents, etc. The unimaginable point unknown to most people is that the devil with all his craftiness sends an idea into our mind. This idea might be called **seed** which would determine its role after germinating.

The message (seed) is first received by the conscious mind. This is where the need or the desire is being stated. What is decided by the conscious mind would create the criteria (information or ideas) that will be used in the sub-conscious mind before connecting it to the Universal Mind. Therefore, if our conscious thought is evil, the universal knowledge and power would now create the ideas and the means of achieving those goals. Remember, the Wise Man says, *"The way a man thinks is who he is"* – ***Proverbs 23:7.***

We as created natural beings do not have the power to over-power the devil as he is the most intelligent creature from God. We should beware of the devil as sometimes he pretends to be good by transforming himself into an angel of light – **2nd Corinthians 11:14.** Most appealing to him is to get people to believe that he simply does not exist; that is to say, hiding under disguise and misguide others.

Because of the joy Jesus would be enjoying when He sits on the right hand side of our Father in Heaven, Satan's intelligence led him to tempt Jesus where he (the devil) thought he has the greatest chance of falling Jesus.

The Bible records in **Matthew Chapter 4** that as Jesus has just fasted for 40 days and nights, Jesus was very hungry but filled with the Holy Spirit.

The first temptation was that if you know you are the Son of God, turn this stone to bread so that you might not die of hunger. Jesus, putting the Holy Spirit in Him to work, then said, "It has been written, Man shall not live and be upheld and sustained by bread alone, but by every word that proceeds out of God's mouth" – Matthew 4:3, 4. Please, compare Deuteronomy 8:3.

To buttress his intelligence, he told Jesus what has been written that must come to pass – **please, read Psalm 91.** These are the words of Satan: *"If you the Son of Man could roll yourself down this mountain, you will not be hurt as God's angels would raise you up."* Then, Jesus replied him, *"On the other hand, it is written also, You shall not tempt, test thoroughly, or try exceedingly the Lord your God." – Matthew 4:6, 7. Please, compare Deuteronomy 6:16.*

To crown it all, the devil knew that with the things of the world, he can influence us as crafty as he is. Remember, *Romans 12:2 says, "That we should no longer conform to the things of the world, but be transformed by renewing our minds. Then, we will be able to test and approve what God's will is – His good, pleasing and perfect will."*

Jesus, taken up the mountain and shown all he has as his kingdom, he tried to influence Jesus by promising Him half of the kingdom if only the **Son of Man** could just bow down before him. Jesus swiftly replied by saying, ***"Get behind me you Satan! Thou shall not worship other gods except the Father that lives in Heaven."*** Immediately, the devil left, and angels came and ministered to Him. **Please, compare Matthew 4:8-11; Deuteronomy 6:13; Exodus 20:4.and James 4:7.**

Here, the lesson that we could deduce from the temptation of Christ by the devil is that, we should never in any circumstance listen and obey Satan's words of deceit; rather, we should at all times listen and obey God's words of fulfillment. For the one that you obey is your master. Please, read Romans 6:16.

TODAY'S HAPPENINGS

From the preceding scenario, there is no one who would not be tempted by the devil; because he roars to and fro the earth seeking whom to devour. Whenever we are seeing things contrary to the ways of God, we should try to find out the source. Thus, the Book of Matthew made us to know that everyone has an evil day – **Matthew 6:34.** In the light of these, the Holy Book tells us never to give the devil a foothold – **Ephesians 4:27**. Remember, everything we do has purpose.

Matthew 26:41 says, "All of you must keep awake (give strict attention, be cautious and active) and watch and pray, that you may not come (and fall) into temptation. The Spirit indeed is willing, but the flesh is weak." Today, immorality has culminated to a very high degree in our society. Children, under the age of puberty became promiscuous to sexual activity through technological advancement.

Furthermore, the internet world with pornographic activities is becoming the biggest trade in the world, as the entire world is influenced through globalization. Almost all advertisements on the television screens connote one pornographic story or the other. Now, because of the money involved, mothers sponsor their under-aged female children to participate in internet nude shows.

In addition, a biological father will be allowed to seduce his eight-year-old daughter to sex, either through the influence of alcohol, chemical drugs, or otherwise. What would be the psychological state of the abused daughter? These are some of the ways the devil can insinuate displeasure into our systems.

In the world today, certain governments pass into laws that allow homosexuality and lesbianism. God knew all these before He took a rib from Adam to make Eve. More deadly, is the heterogeneous sexual activity that happens between man and animal. Incurable sicknesses, giving birth to irregular human structures, and so on, have been on the increase in a world known to be scientifically and medically improved. Why? This is a question we should answer individually. **Please, compare 1st Corinthians 6:9, 10; Exodus 22:19.**

Prophet Isaiah says, **"Therefore, My people will go into captivity [to their enemies] without knowing it and because they have no knowledge [of God]. And their** honourable men [their glory] are famished, and their common people are parched with thirst" – Isaiah 5:13. Unfortunately, many people are already dwelling in these despicable conditions, unknown to them.

If we can read and know exactly our future, why do we not wait until it comes to be? Apart from several books written on astrology, also are public televisions display programme, explaining how someone will live in the future. Today, in most public places, there are installed machines where one can personally read one's horoscope. If they are correct, why do we have these words? – **"When man proposes, God disposes!"** Consequently, this spirit of spiritism used by the devil to deprive God's children of their joy should be worked against. **Please, compare Acts 19:19, 20.**

After we have been created, we were made to have dominion over all that have been created. We should have the earth and subdue it – **Genesis 1:28.** The same Book says that, *"Though heavens and earth will pass away, but the word of God will never pass away until it achieves its purpose"* – **Isaiah 55:11. Please, compare Matthew 5:18.** Why can't we ask ourselves why we are not having the life as given by God? If we search our minds, we shall always find something reasonable to serve as an answer.

Since all have sinned and are falling short of the glory of God, His hand is now becoming too short to save us as well as His ear is becoming too dull to hear us. That is to say, our iniquities have made separation between us and our God, and our sins have hidden His face from us, so that He will not hear when we call on Him. **Please, compare Romans 3:23; Isaiah 59:1, 2.** Endeavouring to educate us, Apostle Paul asked: *"What shall we say [to all this]? Are we to remain in sin in order that God's grace* *(favour and mercy) may multiply and overflow?"* – **Romans 6:1.**

THE DEFEATS OVER SATAN

It has been established that lack of knowledge would lead people astray; and is as a result of ignorance. Therefore, it is worthwhile to sometimes be inquisitive in knowing something about self and the world.

One of the ignorance of most people is that they do not know that we are in this world to fight for our lost rights, which was given to us when Christ was nailed onto the Cross. This fight is to claim what the enemy had denied us of in our respective lives.

At this juncture, it is pertinent to know that we are not fighting against flesh and blood, but against principalities that operate in darkness, evil powers that act against spiritual forces in heavenly realms. Therefore, we must put on the full armour of God to be able to overcome these powers of darkness – Ephesians 6:11, 12.

Now, to be able to do that, the question that comes to mind is, 'do we believe in God, our Creator?' If we believe, how are we responding to His commands? If we have the thought that there is no building that stands firm without a foundation, then we should also know that without a Creator, we wouldn't have been created.

Because of the flow of the evil spirits, we are engaged in a fight which seems to have no end. This fight will persistently be in place only when we think of handling it with our strength. For the Bible says, *"Lean not on your own understanding, but put all your trust, care, and undertakings upon Him, and He will watch over you exceedingly and carefully"* – *Proverbs 3:5-7.* In addition, Exodus 14:14 says, "My God will fight for me, and I will have my peace."

Happily enough, we now know that *"Though we are in the world, we are not of the world" – so says the Bible. He who lives in us is greater than what is in the world – 1st John 4:4.* The power which Jesus used to overcome all temptations was the Holy Spirit in Him. **Please, compare John 14:26; Isaiah 11:1, 2.** This is the same Spirit He left with us when He went to the throne. This also is the same Spirit He used in rising from the grave after three days. Therefore, we should use the **'Anointing Spirit'** given to us by the Father through Jesus – **John 14:17**. This Spirit sends the devil fleeing from you. **Note it: The devil has to flee, not you running away from the devil! Please, compare James 4:7.**

In addition, 2nd Corinthians 10:3-5 encourage us in this manner: "For though we walk (live) in the flesh, we are not carrying on our warfare according to the flesh and using mere human weapons. For the weapons of our warfare are not physical [weapons of flesh and blood], but they are mighty before God for the overthrow and destruction of strongholds. [Inasmuch as we] refute arguments, theories, reasonings and every proud and lofty thing that sets itself up against the [true] knowledge of God; and we lead every thought and purpose away captive into the obedience of Christ (the Messiah, the Anointed One)." **Please, compare 1st Samuel 17:45, 50.**

Here, it is pertinent to know that biblical quotations need not be studied literally. They are God-breathed-inspired prophecies and carry spiritual impartations. They should be taken as spiritual words and studied in that manner. Looking into the preceding quotation, stronghold means obstacles, disappointments, ignorance, failures, sicknesses, etc.

In the light of these, some of the powerful weapons needed to overthrow and destroy all strongholds are having **faith in God through Christ, loving others as one loves oneself, and praying ceaselessly to God in all your undertakings.** Remember, from the days of John the Baptist until the present time, the kingdom of heaven has endured violent assault, and violent men seize it by force [as a precious prize – a share in the heavenly kingdom is sought with most ardent zeal and intense exertion] – **Matthew 11:12.**

Primarily, this kingdom of God is an assertion of God's power in action. Therefore, the fundamental criterion needed to enter into this [Holy] kingdom (having God's power), is to repent and believe the Gospel. Here, if you reason with me, we may agree that the **"Gospel" comprises the word of God, the baptism of Christ, and the death of Christ on the Cross of Calvary.** Happily enough, *Christ testifies, "But if it is by the Spirit of God that I drive out demons, then the kingdom of God has come upon you [before you expected it]"* – Matthew 12:28.

Yes, we have to be fully armed with God's strength in order to overcome the devil's plot. This is done by holding steadfastly to God through Christ. Rest all your anxieties, worries, circumstances, etc, upon Him; for He is the only One who can help bring our enemies under our feet. **Please, read Psalm 108:12, 13; 1st Peter 5:7.**

Because of the mercifulness of God, those who has failed to use the first rain, He would send the latter rain which will retrieve their lost glory and double their blessings. **Please, compare Joel 2:23-27; Job 42:10-17.**

From our practical analysis so far, we should be able to know that there is God who has given us all what to do in order for His word to come true in our lives. Apostle Paul ascertains, *"We are assured and know that [God being a partner in their labour] all things work together and are [fitting into a plan] for good to those and for those who love God and are called according to [His] design and purpose"* – *Romans 8:28.* If we love Him, we will obey His commandments. If we just decide to agree with Him and follow His rules, we will have blessings to the full until it overflows.

To be able to defeat the enemy, we have to use His powerful word which is as sharp as a surgeon's scalpel, cutting through everything; whether doubt or defence, laying us open to listen and obey. Nothing is impervious to God's word. **Please, compare Hebrews 4:12.** Since what we do have its decision from the mind, therefore, we should open up our hearts and allow God to have it. That will make us to believe in His principles and do likewise.

The question that might arise here is that **"what is evil?"** Emphatically, the Bible tells us that anything contrary to His is evil. **Please, compare 1st Corinthians 6:9, 10.** Though, no one is fully holy; however, if we align our understanding with the laid down rules of our Lord Jesus Christ, we will come to know the honour of being virtuous in living.

In that light, if we focus on what is virtuous, moral, etc, we will be able to overcome what negative thoughts our heart(s) receive, through emotions and feelings. And this in turn would make the mind(s) to create the ideas needed to walk in it and be in God. **Please, read Philippians 4:8.**

In this wise, when we receive any message, it is now left for us to allow the Spirit in us does the work. This Holy Spirit is the super-natural spirit that supersedes all other spirits. The Bible says, *"Beloved, Do not put faith in every spirit, but prove (test) the spirits to discover whether they proceed from God; for many false prophets have gone forth into the world" – 1st John 4:1.* **Please, compare Mark 13:21, 22.** Moreover, we are not given a spirit of timidity, or fear; rather, a spirit of discipline, knowledge, and sound mind. When we try to do it on our own, we might be caught in an abyss of calamity. **Please, compare 2nd Timothy 1:7.**

Many people would always believe that their intelligence would sail them through. Even if their knowledge may earn them wealth (money), it may take away their joy, peace, or otherwise. For prosperity includes enough education, spiritual awareness, freedom, health, sleep, peace of mind, time to play and to enjoy family and friends. Prosperity means being filled with enthusiasm for life, filled with spontaneous joy and appreciation. Now, with these known characteristics, are we really prosperous?

Yes, our God so love the world so much that He sent His only begotten Son to the Cross for our sins. **Please, compare John 3:16.** This is the same unconditional love He has for us by creating every individual with potentials and talents. These in-built potentials are the materials one needs to reach one's destiny. **Please, read 2nd Timothy 1:9.**

As long as one remains ignorant in detecting these ingredients in self, one is like a sheep without shepherd. The person will be doing everything to make a living. This time, the potentials to make God's plans to work in our lives remain dormant – not able to flow.

God's plan for us is in the Spirit. As the Holy Spirit searches our hearts (because our hearts is full of evil – **Jeremiah 17:9**) and removes everything that is not of God, He (Spirit) replaces it with the plan He (Spirit) heard from God, about our personal life, before the creation of the world; before we came into our mothers' wombs. Besides, our lives have been predestined. As long as we are in Spirit, walking in the Light (Jesus Christ), and showing unconditional love to all (even to those suspected to be enemies), God – the merciful Father will restore all our lost glories, in the light of these. **Please, compare Romans 8:27, 28.**

Because of the tactics used by the devil, one may undermine these ingredients; and prosperity, according to God's plans, will and purpose may not abound. One of the ways of undermining these ingredients is by comparing oneself to those living without visions. Then, this makes most of us to be struggling to make it through the hard way.

The Wise Man says, *"Life and death lie in our tongues"* – *Proverbs 18:21*. When we say 'life', we mean everything that makes living most pleasurable and admirable; such as wisdom, riches, knowledge, joy, etc, (collectively known as blessings). These are what we are to think about and voice out. On the other hand, death, which does not actually mean physical death; but spiritual death where sicknesses, poverty, ignorance, unhappiness, etc, (collectively known as curses), should not be thought about, neither should it be voiced out. The words that come out of our mouth are like seeds. When they fall, they germinate. So, endeavor to claim fulfilment with your mouth. Here, *Isaiah 45:7 says, "I form the light and create darkness, I make peace [national well-being] and I create [physical] evil (calamity); I am the Lord who does all these things."*

Most unfortunately, believers do not know that as they pray to God for everything, so also the devil look unto God for whatever he needs. Because of his behaviour in heaven, he was chased out from there, and he then decides to use his crafty nature to devour the children of God. What makes us different from him is the "anointing" to move in the Spirit. **Please, compare James 2:19; Mark 5:41; 7:34; Revelation 12:17; Job 2:1-10.**

Therefore, if we allow the Holy Spirit to work in us by surrendering our lives to Him, and walking in diligence, we would be able to know that one can be a businessman, instead of nagging oneself acquiring a degree certificate in medicine. At the end, one's destiny would be achieved. On the contrary, as we try to do it ourselves, we might be walking without knowing our destination. In reality, it takes the will of God to pull out one's potentials, and fruitful them to benefit others and self.

The authority which the Almighty Father has used in creating the world has been given to us. The power which Christ used in ascending the throne has been given to us. **Please, compare Matthew 28:18 and Luke 10:18, 19.** To buttress this unconditional love, Jesus was now sent to be the 'sacrificial lamb' that would serve as atonement (bridging the gap between man and God).

Do we believe in Jesus and agree to follow His principles? For those who see and believe shall inherit the kingdom of God. Also, for those who never saw (like me) but believed shall be saved. For no one shall see the Father except through Jesus. He is the Way, Truth, Life and Light to mankind. **Please, compare John 20:29; John 14:6.**

Dear readers, the only thing the devil cannot take away from us is the Jesus Christ (Holy Spirit) in us. If we allow the Spirit of our Lord Jesus Christ and His Peace He left with us (when He was ascending to the throne in Heaven) to work, not only will we overcome the devil; but also overflow in God's blessings.

In putting this Spirit into full utility, we have to entertain long-suffering principle. We all know what happened to Job, Joseph and Christ to mention but three. In perseverance, patience and endurance, God's plans will come to be according to His will and purpose.

Finally, Christ said: *"He who believes in Me [who cleaves to and trust in and relies on Me] as the Scripture has said, from his innermost being shall flow [continuously] springs and rivers of living water" – John 7:38.* The continuous flow of the living water is the testimony of the Holy Spirit; which is the [new] life in man. When you allow Him (i.e. Holy Spirit) to flow by being in obedience and accordance with God's divine principles, you will overcome the devil at all times. **Please, compare 1st Corinthians 10:13.**

In conclusion, be strong in the Lord [be empowered through your union with Him]; draw your strength from Him [that strength which His boundless might provides] – Ephesians 6:10.

Now, we have detected the tricks of the devil over the earth. Then, let us know the plans which our God has for us to **Walk in the Light** of fulfillment.

CHAPTER FOUR

GOD'S PLAN IS NOT MAN'S PLAN

"For I know the thoughts and plans that I have for you, says the Lord, thoughts and plans for welfare and peace and not for evil, to give you hope in your final outcome." Confirming it, David comments, by requesting from God: "Give us aid against the enemy, for the help of man is worthless. Through and with God we shall do valiantly, for He it is Who shall tread down our adversaries." Please, compare Jeremiah 29:11; Psalm 108:12, 13.

Now, read what Apostle Paul says in 2nd Timothy 1:9: "[For it is He] Who delivered and saved us and called us with a calling in itself holy and to holiness [to a life of consecration, a vocation of holiness]; [He did it] not because of anything of merit that we have done, but because of and to further His own purpose and grace (unmerited favour) which was given us in Christ Jesus before the world began [eternal ages ago]."

Because of God's mercies, Ezekiel 36:26, 27 say; "A new heart will I give you and a new spirit will I put within you, and I will take away the stony heart out of your flesh and give you a heart of flesh. And I will put my Spirit within you and cause you to walk in My statutes, and you shall heed My ordinances and do them."

Yes, the entrance and unfolding of God's words give light; their unfolding gives understanding (discernment and comprehension) to the simple. Therefore, I will continue to honour God and humble myself before Him so that He will establish my steps and direct them by [means of] His word; let not any iniquity have dominion over me. Amen! Please, compare Psalms 119:130, 133."

In the light of these, Prophet Isaiah sealed it up by revealing God's heart to mankind: God says, "I am the Lord, and there is no one else; there is no God besides me. I will gird and arm you, though you have not known Me" – Isaiah 45:5.

Apostle Paul finally concludes that episode in Romans 2:4: "Or are you [so blind as to] trifle with, presume upon, despise and underestimate the wealth of His kindness, forbearance, longsuffering, and patience? Are you unmindful or actually ignorant [of the fact] that God's kindness is intended to lead you to repent (to change your mind and inner man to accept God's will)?"

God is not a god of compromise! He can never be mocked. Whatever we sow that only shall we reap – Galatians 6:7. Therefore, He is using every power in His disposal to put us on the safe side of having His full blessings. Please, re-visit Ezekiel 36:27.

Before you and I came into this world, our lives have been predestined. We are just here to run the acting which God has put in us. However, the running of our activities of what God has written for us could be met only when we are in line with Him, through spiritual connection. Moreover, it takes the Spirit of God to pull it out.

Undoubtedly, God has given us potentials! Nevertheless, the only way to find out who we are is to allow the **"Anointing Spirit"** of God to work in us. That is the reason why destiny could be delayed, but never denied.

Because of the joy and fame derived from certain professions, people decided to fall into those fields just to have the name. On the long run, these might not be the areas where they could have majored in. You may be a common businessman doing buying and selling of goods and services; and this will take you to your goal.

Though, man proposes to be one thing or the other, God disposes to allow His will and purpose to be met in the man's life. For the name and prestige derived from being a Civil Engineer, I was bothering my head hard to acquire a certificate in that discipline. Actually, a certificate was received; but I never worked with it professionally.

In fact, the (bitter) truth about it all is that as one reverence with God, everything one supposed to become here on earth would be made light and easy. Remember, His yoke is light and easy for those who are heavily laden. **Please, compare Matthew 11:28-30.** When we say **"light and easy"**, it means, though we may entertain some obstacles in life, we will overcome them all through our leaning on Christ. **Please, compare 1st Corinthians 10:13.**

No man can be illustrious before the Lord unless his conflicts are many. We have to count it all joy when we pass through trials and tribulations; for when we persevere and persistently stand these tests, we will receive the victory crown of life that God has promised to those who love Him. **Please, compare James 1:12.**

The world of hatred has been in existence since creation. That is to say, since the eating of the forbidden fruit by our first earthly parents, thereby knowing what is good and bad. He that does not know how you eat, walk, or do your things may always find it difficult to harm you. However, he that you share the same fellowship with, your supposed bosom friend who knows your movements would know where and how to hurt you. Your best friend could be your worst enemy; as your worst enemy could be your best friend. Consequently, only your friend knows your secret, and could use it for, or against you, in the light of these. **Please, compare Micah 7:6; Ecclesiastes 5:1, 2; John 15:13-15.**

The potentials God gave to Joseph were to have dreams and interpret dreams. Meanwhile, Joseph is the beloved child of the father as he is the first son from his father's beloved wife. So, this made his brothers to hate him. In his first dream, he and his brothers were binding sheaves of corn in the field. Suddenly, Joseph's sheaf stood erect and the other eleven sheaves rounded it and bowed down to it. **Please, compare Genesis 37:7.**

Sometimes, people say that the voice of men is the voice of God; as the words of our elders are words of wisdom! At this juncture, the brothers have started knowing that Joseph will rule over them in the near future. Therefore, the developed hatred has to increase with great contempt.

Again, he had another dream*: "The sun, the moon, and the eleven stars have to bow down before him."* As he told the dream to their father, here the father asked, *"Do you mean that me, your mother, and your brothers have to bow down before you?"* Though, Jacob made no other comment; however, it was in his mind. **Please, compare Genesis 37:9-11.**

Because of this intense hatred, the brothers planned to eliminate Joseph. But God, who supersedes all man's plans, could protect Joseph all through till he became what He has planned for him. **Please, read Matthew Chapter 2 (The Coming of the Wise Men to Baby Jesus; The Flight into Egypt with the Baby Jesus; and The Coming from Egypt to Nazareth with the Baby Jesus), and compare the plan and purpose of God in your life.**

We only see where we are, or what is happening to us at the moment. Why not we look into the past and see some of our sinful deeds; then see how much our heavenly Father has stood for us? Your mother and father may forsake you; but God – the Maker of heavens and earth will always receive you. He is always with us wherever we are. **Please, compare Isaiah 45:5; Psalm 27:10; Isaiah 43:2, 3; 1st Corinthians 10:13.**

One important thing that most of us do not know is the reason for our existence. Our main purpose of our living as the only creature in the image of God is to reverence, worship, and praise our God all our lives – **Isaiah 43:7.** If we can seek His kingdom and His righteousness first; then peace, endless joy, prosperity, wisdom, freedom, love, etc, will be added unto it. **Please, read Matthew 6:33.**

Romans 8:31 says, "What then shall we say to [all] this? If God is for us, who [can be] against us? [Who can be our foe, if God is on our side?]" The purpose and will of God has to be met in every circumstance. Since that of Joseph would not be an exception, Joseph has to pass through some difficulties before knowing exactly where the brothers were. **Please, compare Genesis 37:15-17; Isaiah 41:10; Jeremiah 1:8; Acts 18:10.**

As the brothers saw him from a distance, they conspired: *"Here comes the dreamer. Let us kill him and see how his dreams will come true" – Genesis 37:19, 20.* Then, Reuben, one of the conspirators (brothers) showed some sense of sympathy, by saying, *"Let us not take his life. Don't shed any blood. Let's throw him into this cistern here in the desert, but don't lay a hand on him."* Reuben suggested that in anticipation to rescue their brother (Joseph) to their father. **Please, compare Genesis 37:21, 22.**

Now, the brothers were tired of walking. So, they have to sit and eat. Suddenly, they saw a caravan of Ishmaelites coming from Gilead. Judah, one of the brothers, now said: *"What shall we gain if we kill our brother and cover up his blood? Therefore, let's sell him to the Ishmaelites without laying our hand on him."* At this juncture, the brothers came to a consensus of opinion and sold Joseph for twenty shekels of silver to the Midianite merchants. This was how Joseph came to Egypt, the land of his enemy. **Please, compare Genesis 37:26-28.**

Because of the cruelty of human nature, the brothers refuse to tell Reuben of what they (other brothers) have done to Joseph. As Reuben could not find Joseph in the well he was placed, he took Joseph's robe and tore it into pieces. They agreed to kill a goat, stained the robe with the blood and took it to their father for identification. Their father certified the robe to be his son's robe.

Then, the brothers said to their father: *"Some ferocious animal has devoured Joseph."* Their father (Jacob) believed that story to be true. Therefore, he mourned Joseph for many days. It was in Egypt that Joseph was sold to Potiphar, one of Pharaoh's officials, the captain of the guards. **Please, compare Genesis 37:29-36.**

Joseph had trusted in God and decided never to wave from God's commandments. In that light, Joseph's presence in Potiphar's house became a blessing to him (Potiphar). Consequently, the officer now handed every activity of the household to be controlled by Joseph. Yes, God can bless and have favour with someone else through your reverence.

As the chosen ones, walking in God's divine principles, we must never expect to escape troubles before we could reach our glory. Based on that, Joseph is now being tempted by the wife of Potiphar.

The Holy Book says, *"If we are tempted, we are not being tempted by God; but we could be led by the Spirit to where we could be tempted by the devil."* In the light of these, therefore, falling into sin does not come from circumstances, or otherwise; rather, it is as a result of personal choice. Again, the Book says, *"If we are tempted and fall into sin (temptation), we are being carried away, enticed and baited by our own evil desire (lust, and passion)."* Please, compare James 1:13, 14.

To every situation, there is always a bright side as well as a dark side. It is well for us if, while the flesh mourns over trials, our faith triumphs in divine faithfulness.

Fortunately enough, Joseph stood the test and allow his flesh to mourn and suffer for the sin he has never committed. As Potiphar's wife was trying to seduce him, he ran away in order for the ordinances of God to be met. And this led him to prison as his master's wife told an opposite story to her husband Potiphar.

God's will and purpose must be met in our lives. **Amen!** As at the time we are thinking of something else, we don't know what the Almighty Father has for us spiritually. God can lead us to where our glory could be reached. It is not all tribulations we could attribute to be caused by Satan. God could use it to see how faithful we are with Him and use it to take us to the next level of our glory and prosperity. **Please, take the life of biblical Job as a case study!**

In the prison, two of Pharaoh's guards were there for one offence or the other. As God could make it, they both had dreams which no one could interpret. Actually, there are 'forces' that could work against our God-given potentials; however, with the power of God which keeps all other powers under His, would make our dreams and potentials to be reached. **Amen!**

These dreams were interpreted by Joseph and they came to be how he has told them. One was to regain his position as the cup-bearer of Pharaoh; while the other was to be hung and the birds of the air would use his flesh as food. After three days, there was a feast held by the king, and everything came to pass as it has been said.

Because of man's egocentric attitude, hatred, and envy, the cup-bearer never did what he promised Joseph when he regained his position. He entirely forgot Joseph, and he could die and rot in prison if need be. The Bible says, ***"Put your trust in no man, or princes; only put all your hope in our Lord Almighty" – Psalm 118:8, 9.***

Every disappointment is a blessing, as most of us believe! To make His will and purpose to be met in the life of Joseph, He **'planted'** a dream in Pharaoh which the land's dream interpreters could not interpret. Again, when your way pleases God, your enemies would be at peace with you. **Please, compare Proverbs 16:7.** The cup-bearer now remembers Joseph as the only person who could interpret the dream.

At this juncture, Joseph, though, a foreigner and a prisoner in Egypt, was brought to Pharaoh to do the interpretation. He did it, giving the advantages and disadvantages; and how the situation could be managed against famine in the land of Egypt.

As king Pharaoh heard that, then, he decided: *"If no one could interpret this dream other than you, it means that you have got the ability and capability to handle the situation."* For this reason, Joseph was granted amnesty and became a governor in the land of his enemy. And as a governor, he became in-charge of food in Egypt.

Note: Joseph was always putting God first in all his doings, including the interpretations of dreams. Please, compare Genesis 40:8; 41:16.

Now, there is famine in Israel. Jacob, the father of Joseph and his family has no food to eat. The other children have to come to Egypt to get food for the household. Remember, the brothers of Joseph have lied to their father that Joseph has been killed by a wild animal. Then, Jacob mourned his beloved son and bored it all. So, without doubt, Jacob believed that Joseph is dead.

When the brothers of Joseph came to Egypt, Joseph could recognise his brothers; but the brothers not. Before Joseph could give them food, he asked them of their father and his junior brother (Benjamin). They told him with trembling that they are at home. Joseph told them not to be afraid. He demanded for their father and the junior brother by sending some of them home with food, and the rest withheld.

As they came with their father and junior brother, Joseph asked them if they know him. They answered **'No.'** Joseph told them that he is their brother sold to the Egyptian slave trader sometime ago. **And that they thought evil against him, but God meant it out for good to save lives. Please, compare Genesis 50:20.**

Furthermore, for whatever we are doing, vengeance is not ours; but God's – **Psalm 94:1; Romans 12:19.** So, Joseph forgives his brothers what they have done against him when they were young. They were so devilish to him because he told them of the dreams he had when they were young.

If we trust in man, we shall always have what is of man; likewise, if we trust in God, we will have the blessings of God. When we say 'trust', we mean the ability to have 'full confidence' in what we believe in.

The Bible says, *"Because of the Lord's great love we are not consumed, for His compassions never fail. They are new every morning; great and abundant is Your stability and faithfulness. Furthermore, the Lord is good to those who wait hopefully and expectantly for Him, to those who seek Him; it is good to wait quietly for the salvation of the Lord" – Lamentations 3:22, 23, 25, 26.*

Now, let us recall Daniel's story we read in **Chapter Two** of this book. Because of the trust Daniel has for God, he obeyed His commandments. The excellent Spirit in Daniel has no fear of any man or thing. Moreover, Daniel honoured God by obeying the law which states that we should not have any other god before Him. Yes, we are supposed to love God first before any other man or thing. **Please, compare Daniel 6:3; Exodus 20:3-5.**

Therefore, ***Nahum 1:7 says, "The Lord is good, a Strength and Stronghold in the day of trouble; He knows (recognizes, has knowledge of, and understands) those who take refuge and trust in Him."***

Without doubts, man can plan any havoc against man. But if you do not lean on your own understanding, only on God you rest all your hope; apart from protecting you from all adversaries, also, He will in due season crown you with the victory crown which He has promised those that love Him.

Jesus says, **"Do not let your hearts be troubled (distressed, agitated). You believe in, adhere to, trust in, and rely on God; believe in, adhere to, trust in, and rely also on Me. In My Father's house, there are many dwelling places (homes). If it were not so, I would have told you; for I am going away to prepare a place for you" – John 14:1, 2.** With this, He meant that if one rests all ones needs, worries, plans, thoughts, etc, on Him, one has overcome the world. **Please, compare John 9:31.**

Apostle Paul in **Galatians 5:6 says, "For [if we are] in Christ Jesus, neither circumcision, nor un-circumcision counts for anything, but only faith activated, energized, expressed, and working through love."**

With God's kindness, God gave us faith through Abraham's faith, and bestowed righteousness [grace (undeserved gift)] onto us through Christ death on the Cross. And the only thing God needs from us is to love others as you have loved yourself. **Please, compare Romans 4:16, 17; Ephesians 2:8, 9; John 14:21, 23.**

At this juncture, some of the characteristics, properties, or elements needed to show that one is giving out love as needed are **good character, speeches or discussions that edify others, helping from the heart without prejudices, etc.** Possessing these moral etiquettes will make you to help your enemy when he/she may be in need. **Please, compare Romans 12:19-21.** Having been able to walk in these precepts, then we can wait for God's answer to our requests. Remember, God can never be mocked; for whatever one sows, thou shall he reap – **Galatians 6:7**

Immeasurably, Philippians 4:8 appeals, "For the rest, brethren, whatever is true, whatever is worthy of reverence and is honourable and seemly, whatever is just, pure, lovely and lovable, whatever is kind, winsome, and gracious, if there is any virtue and excellence, if there is anything worthy of praise, think on and weigh and take account of these things [fix your mind on them]."

Reawakening the verse, **John 9:31:** the one who hears God, and obeys them would have thoughts of responsibility; while the one who disobeys would have thoughts of liability. **Please, compare John 14:21, 23.**

When we say **"Thoughts of Responsibility"**, we mean fruitful thoughts that could be developed to take us to the desired goal. **"Thoughts of Liability"** are the evil thoughts that bring to man great perplexity (doubts, frustration, fear, etc.) However, your thoughts of responsibility could turn to thoughts of liability when your goals are not properly chosen and adequately focussed.

Happily enough, in **John 14:21,** Christ reminds us that, **"The person who has His commands and keeps them is the one who [really] loves Him; and whoever [really] loves Him will be loved by His Father and He [too] will love him and will show (reveal, manifest) Himself to him [He will let Himself be clearly seen by him and make Himself real to him]."**

In summary, God, who has His fruitful thoughts and plans for mankind, even before man was created, would manifest in those who loved Christ.

In conclusion, [most] blessed is the man who believes in, trust in, and relies on the Lord, and whose hope and confidence the Lord is. For he shall be like a tree planted by the waters that spreads out its roots by the river; and it shall not see and fear when heat comes; but its leaf shall be green. It shall not be anxious and full of care in the year of drought, nor shall it cease yielding fruit. Please, read Jeremiah 17:7, 8.

Herstellung und Verlag:
BoD - Books on Demand, Norderstedt
ISBN 978-3-7386-3023-7